The authors would like to thank the following for their help with this book: Richard Ames, Flying Tiger Associates; Chandos E. Bush III, kite builder and model; Jeanne Bush; Bill Everett, kite flying expert; Vic Heredia, Vic's Fighter Kites; Chris Kampe, kite tester; Gloria and Charles Lugo, Let's Fly A Kite; Stratton Air Engineering; Ivan Toney, kite manufacturer; Tyrus Wong, kite flying expert; Eric Zimmerman, kite flying expert.

BETTER KITE FLYING
for Boys and Girls

Ross R. Olney and Chan Bush

DODD, MEAD & COMPANY · NEW YORK

PICTURE CREDITS

Photographs on the following pages are used by permission and through the courtesy of: Ross R. Olney, 16, 32; Stratton Air Engineering, 13 (left), 41, 42. All other photographs are by Chan Bush.

796.15
O
cop.2
5.95

1 2 3 4 5 6 7 8 9 10

Library of Congress Cataloging in Publication Data

Olney, Ross Robert, 1929-
    Better kite flying for boys and girls.

    Summary: Discusses notable kite feats, how a
kite flies, how to fly it, kite styles and types, building a
kite, safety, and kite fighting, a national pastime in
some countries.
    1. Kites—Juvenile literature. [1. Kites] I.
Bush, Chan, joint author. II. Title.
TL759.5.O42   796.1′5   80-14817
ISBN 0-396-07853-2

CONTENTS

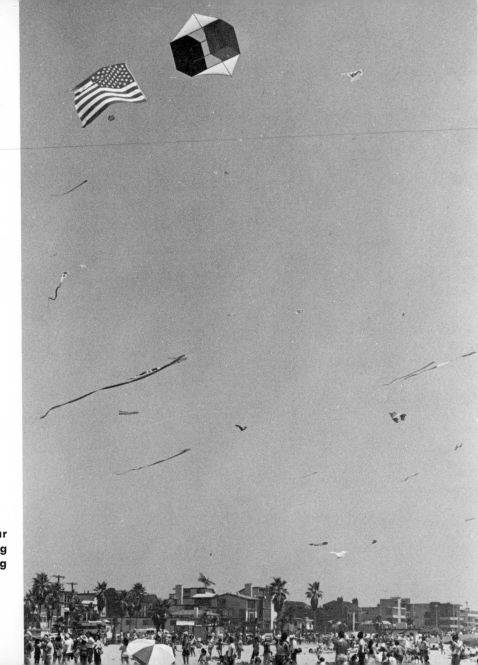

Kite flying, more popular every day, is an exhilarating experience for both young people and adults.

ABOUT KITES

In 1753 a Russian scientist decided to try to duplicate the famous kite experiment of the American, Benjamin Franklin. Franklin had succeeded with his experiment the year before. Almost everybody had heard that Ben was able to draw electricity from the sky by flying a kite during a thunderstorm.

Franklin and his twenty-one-year-old son, William, had gone into a field outside of Philadelphia just as the storm was brewing. They had with them a kite made of a common silk handkerchief. Franklin put his kite into the air and at first nothing happened. Then he noticed that the fuzzy loose strands of the hemp string were standing out. This told him that electricity was present.

He had attached a house key to the string with a silk ribbon, so that he would not be in contact with the wet string. Sure enough, an electric spark jumped from the key to his finger.

Nobody else was there to see the experiment because Ben and his son feared that witnesses would make fun of them if it failed.

The Russian scientist didn't fail either. In fact, he succeeded in a tragic way. He flew his kite in a thunderstorm and was electrocuted. There were no safety rules for kite flying then, but now the very first one is: "Never fly your kite in the rain or near storm clouds."

Kites have been flown by man for centuries—for fun, to ward off evil spirits, for military purposes, for science. They have been used to measure high-altitude temperatures and pressures, to send men aloft as observers, and to help with construction work. They have been used to drop messages, to train pilots, and to lift radio antennas. Kites have also been used to lift cameras for aerial photography.

Kites have even been used in courts of law to determine guilt or innocence. The judge would fly a kite over those suspected of a crime. Where the kite dipped down was important, since that indicated the guilty party. Punishment followed swiftly, for the kite was thought to be divinely guided and nobody wanted to argue with the gods. Except, perhaps, the "guilty" person. But that was hundreds of years ago. Fortunately, courts no longer use this system.

As late as 1914, Charles M. Miller, a Los Angeles school official, suggested that kites might indicate the future of a young student. In his book, *Kitecraft and Kite Tournaments*, he said, "The string is often a source of great annoyance. It snarls up and some lads will cut out the hard knots, but others will tackle the knotty problems and untangle them. They will do the same with knotty problems in life later on."

Kite flying is thought to have originated in China. Over 2,000 years ago the Chinese were flying kites with whistles, vibrating strings, and other musical

Dragon kites have always been popular in China and Japan. This is a huge modern-day one—being launched, and in flight.

devices. In fact, their name for the kite—*feng cheng*—means "wind harp." In 200 B.C., the Chinese general, Han-Hsin, flew a kite to the wall of an enemy palace so that he could measure the exact distance. Then he used the measurement to determine how far to dig a tunnel to the wall and under it, so that his men could enter the palace and overpower the enemy emperor.

Kites and kite flying spread to other Eastern countries—to Japan, Malaya, Thailand, India—and then to Europe and the Western World. Kites became a part of legends, traditions, and celebrations. In some countries thousands of men, women, and children fly kites in massive displays during kite festivals. Children in Tibet learned to tie heavy kites to their waists when they rode their ponies. Soon they would be going fast enough to be lifted from their saddles for a short flight. They were the world's first "hang gliders."

Kite fighting developed in Eastern countries, too. The sport still remains quite popular in China, Japan, Malaya, India, and Korea. It is growing rapidly in popularity in the United States today.

Flying a kite demands no great skill, relatively small expense, and minor physical exertion. Kites are flown for the simple, exhilarating fun of the activity. The calming influence of the gentle tug on the string and the bright object in the sky has worked like magic down through the ages. Kite

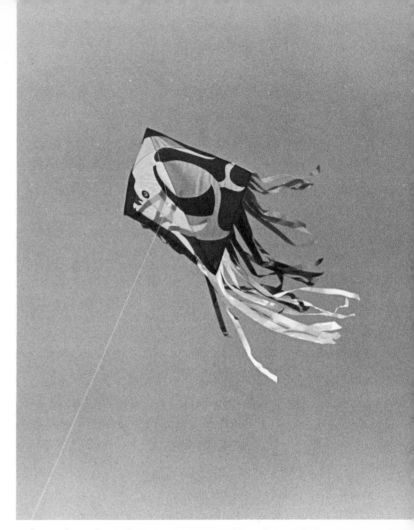

Fighting kites have become very popular. The added streamers would be removed for fighting.

9

flying is pure enjoyment. It doesn't have to be anything else.

But it has been. Kites have been put to work for many purposes. Ben Franklin wasn't the only one to experiment with kites. By the nineteenth century, kites were a solid tool of scientists and inventors. Alexander Wilson, a Scottish astronomer, used kites to carry thermometers aloft to measure temperatures at high altitudes. An English scientist tied anemometers to kites to determine wind speeds at various altitudes. About 1825, another Englishman named George Pocock attached two huge kites to a carriage and his vehicle moved along at the breakneck speed of 25 miles per hour. He called his system a "Charvolant," from the French words for "kite" (*cerf volant*) and "carriage" (*char*). Pocock also experimented with lifting people into the air with kites, and was one of the first to document the fact that the wind is generally stronger and steadier at higher altitudes.

During the Boer War (1899–1902), trains of hexagonal kites were used for spotters high over the front. A brave soldier would mount a specially built frame and ride the kites up and over the enemy lines. Then he would be pulled back down to report.

Alexander Graham Bell, inventor of the telephone, was interested in kites as potential flying machines. About 1893, Lawrence Hargrave of Australia had developed the box kite, and in the early 1900s Bell was experimenting with mammoth

There are more and more kite stores around the United States. This is Let's Fly A Kite in Marina del Rey, California.

kites 40 feet long that would lift men.

The Wright brothers were originally kiters, using kites to test many of their theories before they themselves flew in the first airplane. They had many hundreds of flights in glider-like kites. They even flew their original heavier-than-air machine at the end of tow ropes before they mounted the engine and took to the air.

It was a boy's kite that took the first line across the gorge at Niagara Falls when the great suspension bridge was built. The river was clogged with ice and workmen had no way to get the first cable across. So the chief engineer offered a reward of $10 to anyone who could fly a kite to the other side.

Homan Walsh, a young boy, took up the challenge. He flew his small kite across and caused it to land. There workmen fastened a very light line to the kite string. This line was hauled back across, where a heavier line was attached. Back and forth went the lines, heavier and heavier, until the first steel cable could be drawn across. Homan got his ten dollars, and kites had been put to work in the construction industry.

During the Civil War, kites were put to a novel use. Commanders needed a way to offer amnesty to Confederate troops willing to surrender. Special two-stringed kites were sent far over the Rebel lines. One string was strong, the other weak. High up on the weak string a bundle of leaflets promising good treatment to prisoners was attached.

When the kite reached the proper spot over the Rebels, the strong string was slackened and this put all the strain on the weak string. At that instant the weak string would break, releasing the proclamations. In the prose of one magazine of the day, they fell "thick as autumnal leaves."

The first woman to fly in a kite was Almenia Rice, a circus performer. In a kind of box kite with wings, Almenia "flew" from the roof of a building in Boston in 1901, and succeeded in staying aloft for several minutes. Earlier, George Pocock had lifted his young daughter into the air in a chair attached to kite ropes. Meanwhile, Marconi was receiving his first transatlantic radio message from an antenna that had been carried to a height of 400 feet by a box kite.

One of the greatest photographic feats was possible because of a kite. Pictures were needed of the terrible devastation of the San Francisco earthquake of 1906. So George Lawrence attached his huge camera on a string of seventeen kites and obtained the photographs.

In 1941, Francis Rogallo introduced his flexible kite, the Flexikite, which has no rigid frame and flies with shroud lines, much like a parachute. The Flexikite, adjusting to changes in wind force by changing its shape, has been used in NASA experiments and is responsible for modern hang gliding activity.

Kites were still being used in warfare as late as

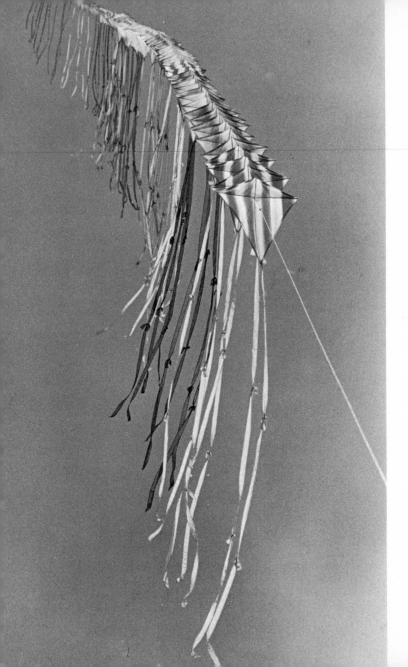

1945 when the Allies discovered that German U-boats had been lifting observers from the turrets of submarines by using a combination kite-helicopter. At that time kites were standard Allied life raft equipment to carry aloft an emergency radio antenna.

Modern kites are now available in a marvelous variety of shapes and sizes and colors. You can buy bumblebees, eagles, and octopus-shaped kites from your local hobby or kite store. These are easy to assemble and easy to fly. Dragon kites are sometimes hundreds of feet long. There are kites that look like old-time clipper ships, World War I airplanes, and kits that will give you kite trains with as many kites as you wish.

Kites come in sizes as small as postage stamps (flown on silken threads) and as large as 150 square feet with a pull of more than 300 pounds. (Such a huge one uses special steel wire for its "string.") Kites range in cost from virtually nothing (if built at home with materials found around the house) to a dollar to thousands of dollars. Famous people like Yul Brynner and Robert Redford are kite enthusiasts.

In 1978, a seventeen-year-old boy by the name of Steven Flack flew into kite flying history and into

Kite systems are not as hard to fly as they appear to be. Each kite will fly by itself, or as a part of the train.

Above: The Ghost Clipper is a popular kit kite. Right: A centipede kite in flight.

the *Guinness Book of Records*. Steven, a kite flying enthusiast for more than ten years, decided to go for the altitude record. He wanted to fly a kite higher than anyone is history.

So, on a 25-pound test line with seven kites spaced at 1½-mile intervals, he lofted a kite to an incredible 37,908 feet. The record still stands.

Meanwhile, another record was being set by a Japanese kite flyer from Kamakura. Flying small triangular kites the size of postcards, he managed to loft 4,128 kites on one string. The highest of Kazuhido Asaba's kites was 1,300 meters (4,266 feet) in the sky. Asaba broke a record only one month old set by another Japanese group who flew 3,800 kites on one string.

Records such as these are made to be broken. You might want to try one of them yourself as you learn more about the great fun of kite flying.

HOW A KITE FLIES

A kite is an unpowered device made to be flown in the air at the end of a string or line. It may or may not have a tail, and the tail may or may not be attached for decoration or stabilization.

You'll read more about kite safety in a later section, but did you know that Ben Franklin didn't just go out and fly his kite in the rain without certain precautions? That could be deadly. Instead, he attached a piece of silk ribbon to the hemp string he was using. Then he stood inside the shelter of a shed, remaining dry and on dry ground. Where the silk ribbon was attached to the hemp string, he hung a huge brass key. This was also inside the shed, just at the door.

As electricity built up in the wet hemp string it was insulated from Franklin by the dry silk ribbon. Very cautiously he reached out with a knuckle to brush against the brass key. Only then did harmless sparks jump from the key to his knuckles. He didn't want to face the very real threat of electrocution, should his theories be correct.

But what made his kite stay in the sky in the first place? After all, a kite is a heavier-than-air device.

Airplanes are heavier than air, too, and they stay in the air. They do it the same way a kite does it. An airplane, glider, hang glider, or any other winged, man-carrying machine moves forward in the air by

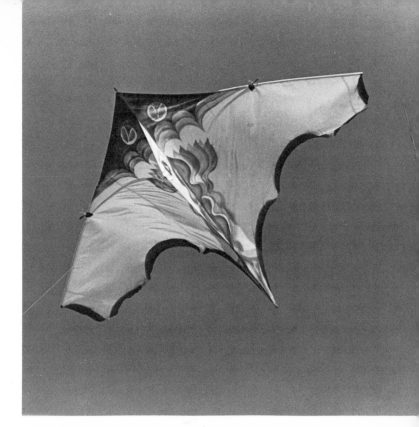

Kites stay aloft by the action of the wind on their surfaces.

means of an engine or glide action. Because of the shape of the wing of an airplane, this forward movement causes a lower pressure of air above the wing than below it. This follows the scientific principles first stated by Daniel Bernoulli of Switzerland in the eighteenth century. When air moves quickly, its pressure decreases; when it moves slowly, its pressure increases. Air passing straight beneath the airfoil shape of an airplane's wing moves more slowly than air curving up and over the upper surface of the wing. Thus, the pressure below is greater than that above the wing. It pushes the wing up and lifts the airplane. Simple, but it works.

A kite does not necessarily move forward in the air, but it also establishes two areas of differing air pressure. A kite lies at an angle to the wind, and the movement of air past the face of the kite causes a lower pressure zone of air behind it. This causes the air below and in front of the kite to push or lift the kite, and it flies.

Regardless of the design of the kite, this low pressure versus higher pressure is what accounts for the kite, which is heavier than air, lifting into the sky. The kite may have wings or some other airfoil shape, or it may have just a series of flat or rounded surfaces, but it all works the same. The principle remains; it simply operates on more than one surface.

Running with your kite will surely create wind around it and cause it to rise, but most experts feel that running is wasted effort. Well-made kites will rise without all that work. Besides, running might make you pay more attention to your feet and less to the kite, resulting in awkward flight.

You can create your own wind for your kite's

Low air pressure versus higher air pressure lifts a kite upward.

A tail on a kite may add stability.

surface to react to by a series of short tugging motions on the string. The tugs move the kite forward toward you. This creates a higher pressure in front of the kite and reduces the air pressure behind it. So the kite moves into the lower pressure space. With each tug the kite moves up higher and higher, and it will remain there as long as the tugs continue.

Most well-balanced kites will fly without a tail. Tails are necessary on some models, but they do add to the weight and drag of any kite.

Did you know that kites can even be lofted and flown indoors? Kite flyer Dinesh Bahadur, a noted kite fighting expert and owner of a chain of kite stores, once flew a kite indoors for a world record, at that time, of 46 minutes and 2 seconds. He did this by keeping the kite in the air with tugging motions.

Generally, though, you will be outside and have the advantage of at least a slight breeze.

THE BRIDLE—If the one handling the string is the "brains" of a kite, then the bridle is certainly the "control panel." The bridle is the means by which the kite is attached to the string. It is a short piece of string that adjusts the angle of the kite to the wind as it is flying. The more a kite is heading squarely into the wind, the faster it will go up.

Remember this rule. The stronger the wind, the shorter the top leg of the bridle should be. This will tend to tip the top of the kite into the wind, allow-

Kite bridles can be simple, as on this three-stick kite
(left), or as complex as the one at right with a rod
attached for a flag.

ing more of the wind to flow past the face of the kite. Practice will improve your technique in bridle adjustment.

Be sure the kite is balanced on its bridle side-to-side by hanging the kite from its bridle before flight to test it. A poorly balanced kite will tend to move to the heavy side, often resulting in a series of dives to that side. You can, of course, put a tail on such an off-balanced kite, but improving the side-to-side balance should make the kite flyable without a tail.

Here's a string weight rule:

1. For paper kites, use 9-pound test line
2. For plastic kites, use 20-pound test line
3. For cloth kites, use 30-pound test line

Kite strings (from left to right): 9-pound test, 30-pound test, 50-pound test, 100-pound test, and 180-pound braided nylon test.

WHERE TO FLY—Pick a spot away from power lines, large trees, and buildings. Not only will these objects capture your kite, but they can also be dangerous to you. Finally, they may create strong currents that will interfere with control.

Kites seem to fly best in winds of from 8 to 12 miles per hour. Wind speeds are not difficult to judge. Here's how:

A. A wind speed of about 5 miles per hour will move tree leaves and can be felt very slightly on your face.

B. A wind speed of about 10 miles per hour will keep leaves in constant motion and move a light flag into action.

C. A wind speed of about 15 miles per hour will move the tops of trees, raise dust, and blow loose paper and other light materials around.

D. A wind speed of about 20 miles per hour will make smaller trees sway.

NOW LET'S LAUNCH—Once you have picked a good spot for flying your kite, you are ready to launch it.

1. Anchor the spool of string so that the string will fall off as you need it, just as a fishing reel allows the line to come off. Many kite flying enthusiasts now use a fishing rod and reel combination specially made for kite flying. You can buy one of these in your local hobby or kite store if you wish.

2. If you have a helper, have him stand holding the kite about 50 feet away, with the top pointing

An open place away from buildings and trees is a good place to fly a kite.

This is a standard reel used by many kite fliers.

up. The wind should be coming from behind you.

3. Pull the string until it is fairly tight, then signal your friend to launch the kite upward. At the same moment, pull in on the string smoothly. The

The correct way to hold a reel while flying a kite.

kite will climb up and away. Just allow the excess line to coil at your feet for the time being. It'll be payed out again soon.

4. As you feel the wind tugging on the kite, slowly let the string out again. A series of in-and-out tugging motions will create even more pressure on the face of the kite and cause it to climb higher into more wind.

5. If the wind is strong enough (but not too strong) you can simply stand with your back to the wind and pay out the string as the kite climbs.

FLYING A KITE—With your kite launched and in the air, you can then maneuver it and control it.

1. The best place for the string is over the tip or just below the tip of your forefinger, giving you the "feel" of the kite flying. Flying a kite is just a matter of pulling in to make the kite rise and paying out to achieve distance and control.

2. If the kite begins to loop or go in the wrong direction, pay out the line. This will cause the kite to stop and float on the wind.

3. When the kite is about fifty feet or so in the air, hold it for a moment. If it flies well without action from you, it is ready to go higher. If you must fight it to control it or if it just falls back to earth, bring it back for bridle adjustments (or even to pick another place, or another day).

4. A diving, constantly looping kite is usually a sign of too much wind, poor design, too short a tail, or a lopsided bridle. Too long a tail will cause

One-stringed models . . . or two-stringed models can be controlled very precisely, as expert Bill Everett (right) demonstrates.

the kite to be sluggish and unable to climb.

5. If your kite won't climb and everything else seems right, bring it back down and shorten the upper leg of the bridle.

6. If your kite continues to loop out of control, or dives repeatedly at the ground, let it get as near the ground as possible, then suddenly let out as much string as you can. This will cause it to land lightly and without damage.

7. Don't ever let the string go with one hand until you have it solidly in the other hand. Both hands should be working with short, even pulls, with your hands close to your chest.

8. Remember that the higher your kite goes, the less control you have. Losing control of the string is the most common mistake kite fliers make, such as allowing the string to lose its tautness. The way to regain control is to tug quickly and rhythmically.

9. The first time you fly a new kite, learn about it at a fairly low altitude. Get to know it. Watch how it moves at the end of the string and be prepared to bring it down for adjustments.

10. To bring your kite down, reel it in slowly until it comes into your hand or very close to the ground. Then let out string to allow it to settle. Once it has landed, hold onto the string to prevent the kite from damaging itself by bouncing along the ground. Never pull the kite to you along the ground

Long kite tails are playful and decorative.

23

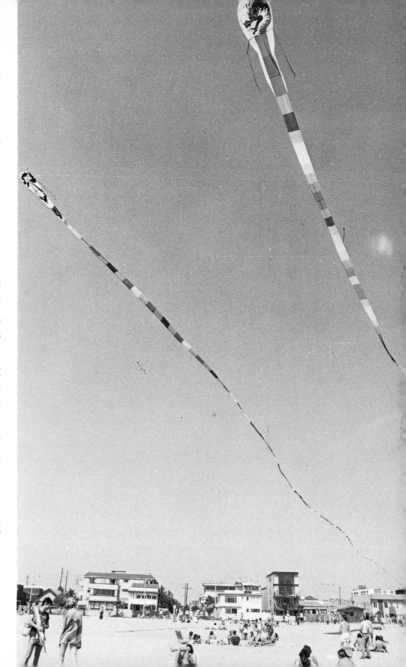

by its string. Have a friend go pick it up while you hold the string, or else reel in the string as you walk toward the kite.

11. Do not allow your kite to fly you. You fly your kite.

Some experts feel that no kite should have a tail. They feel that only amateurs fly a kite with a tail. Others, however, feel that a kite tail is playful and decorative, and a natural part of flying. A tail also adds stability to a slightly unstable kite.

You may come to enjoy very large kites, or very small kites, or both. You may want to fly very high, or to keep your kite low and in sight where you can admire it—or both. Some go for highly decorative kites with rainbow colors and intriguing shapes. Others like standard-shaped kites. Some enjoy fighting kites, while others hate to see a kite crashing.

You'll have to choose, and the field is broad indeed.

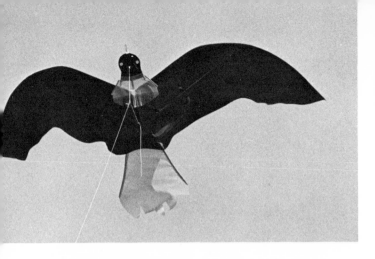

KITE STYLES AND TYPES

There are an astounding number of kites now available in kite stores and hobby shops. Every day kite lovers are designing and building new and different kites. As old as the hobby is, it is still ever-growing and changing. Kite shapes run from amusing to astonishing.

Kites make great gifts, the type that makes people say, "Now, why didn't I think of that?" In the United States there are more than 200 shops devoted exclusively to the sale of kites, and that number continues to grow. This is true even though kite flying is a recent hobby in this country (when compared to the fact that kites have been flown for centuries in other countries). Kites are also available in department stores, hobby shops, and

Kites come in all shapes and sizes. Here is a bird-shaped kite in flight, and an octopus kite.

even in grocery stores. It won't be difficult to find a kite when you decide to buy, build, and fly one.

More than 150,000,000 kites were sold in the United States in 1979 (compared to a mere 40,000,000 in 1970). Kite flying, which never really went away, is here to stay. There are about 25 kite flying clubs, where members gather to talk about kites and fly them. Colleges such as Vassar, Yale, and Princeton have kite teams that regularly compete with each other, and many other colleges are looking at the sport with teams in mind.

History does not record the type of kite that Ishikawa Goyamen used in Japan in the sixteenth century when he attempted to steal gold statues of carp from atop the castle of a nobleman, but there are many, many different types of kites.

FLAT KITES—Also known as diamond kites (though they come in certain other shapes as well), these are usually two-stickers and not very popular anymore. A flat kite is the simplest form of kite— one stick crossing the other about a third of the way from the top—but they have lost ground to the more exotic shapes, and to the bowed Eddy-type kite.

According to many experienced kite fliers, the flat kite is not a very good kite. Many young fliers have been turned away from the sport of kite flying because this is the kite they started with. The flat kite has to have a long tail, it has a poor lift-to-drag ratio, and it seldom flies as high as the more efficient shapes.

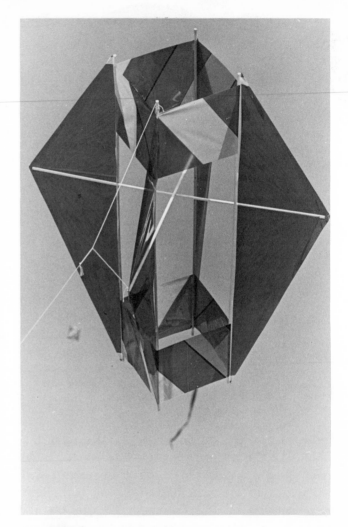

A standard winged box kite.

BOX KITES—The box kite is a three-dimensional box shape considered to be a workhorse type. It has no tail and generally flies well in a strong enough wind. It looks like a rectangular milk carton with the bottom and top cut out, and the midsection missing.

The box kite was invented by Lawrence Hargrave in Australia in 1892, and it has been used by NASA engineers to help develop space vehicles. Because it is very strong, it is the kite that is normally used to carry heavy loads. The Wright brothers used box kites in their early experiments and it was generally a box kite used to loft humans into the air.

Winged box kites are box kites with an attached triangular section on two or all four sides. The wings are like extra flaps—to increase the lift of the kite.

Also included as a box kite type is the tetrahedral kite invented by Alexander Graham Bell. It is made of a series of cells, each of which is composed of four equal triangles. This type of kite is a good climber and very easily controlled.

EDDY-TYPE KITES—The Eddy kite resembles the flat kite, but while it is a two-sticker, the horizontal spar is curved. The two sticks come together more in a "T" shape than a diamond. Easy to fly, the Eddy requires no tail and is a marvelous kite to begin with. Novices quickly learn the techniques of flying with a kite that will almost automatically climb into the sky.

27

A homemade Eddy-type kite.

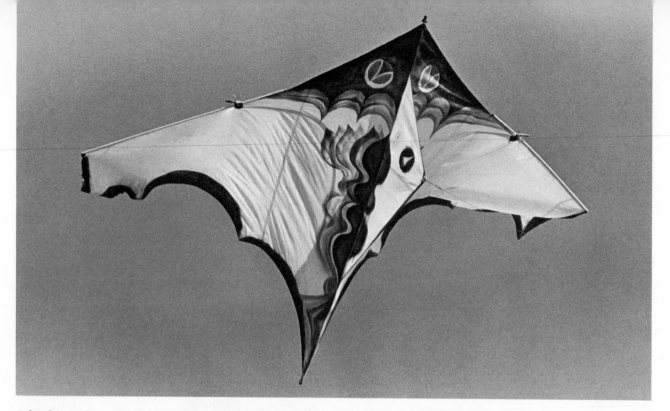

A keel-type kite. The keel replaces the bridle in this common snap-together model.

William A. Eddy was the inventor of the tail-less kite, the kind with a bowed crosspiece. He used this type of kite to make weather observations near Boston as early as 1894.

It is just as easy to make an Eddy kite as a flat, diamond-shaped kite, and you will probably enjoy the results much more. See the next section for building details.

FRAMELESS KITES—The nonrigid kite is the most modern of all kite forms. This type of kite has no wooden or plastic sticks or other stiffeners. It is flown with shroud lines, like a parachute. The Rogallo kite was the forerunner of such modern kites as the parafoil and other nonrigid shapes.

These kites are spectacular to fly, although their price alone might keep them in the expert or experienced class of kite flier. They are often used to carry a load such as a camera or measuring equipment. But, since they are frameless and keel-less, they are long-lasting. A crash won't hurt them as it will a framed or keeled kite.

KEEL KITES—The keel on a keel kite makes it one of the most stable of all kites to fly. These kites are usually triangular or even bird-shaped. They have a single flat surface and use a keel (usually made of whatever the kite covering is) instead of a traditional string bridle. One or more keels act almost the same as the lower fin on a fish, adding great stability and control.

Since keel kites are very easy to fly and require no tail, they are becoming very popular. Chances are if you have recently purchased a bat-shaped kite or one of a number of other bird-shaped kites it is probably a keel-type kite.

SPECIALTY AND SCRATCH-BUILT KITES—There are many new kites appearing on the market every day as the sport continues to gain in popularity. Some of these new shapes do not readily fit into any of the traditional categories, though all are based upon the same characteristics of flight. You can buy kites in the shape of airplanes, birds, clipper ships, frogs, and other exotic shapes.

Fighter kites are becoming very popular, as well as miniatures, and even kites to do work for you

A keel kite going up.

29

(such as fishing). Most of these kites are more difficult to fly, since they may have sacrificed efficiency for beauty or utility. They are often for the more expert kite flying enthusiast.

You can buy "kite systems" consisting of a number of kites to be flown in a train, all linked together (or they can be flown independently of each other). Most kite stores and hobby stores carry these systems and many of the other specialty kites.

There is also a broad array of home-built kites. Take a stick or two, or no sticks at all, an old shower curtain, window shade, apron, or (a fairly modern item that is a bonanza to kite builders) a plastic garbage bag, and use your imagination. Some astounding shapes have been built that fly well in-

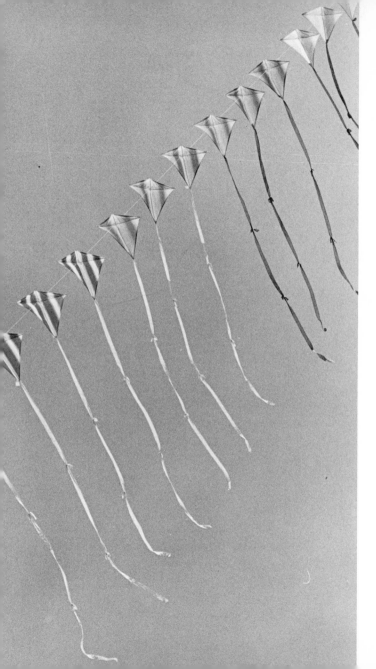

deed. Remember the basic principles of flight that can be observed in any other proven kite and go from there.

Use an old coat hanger for a stiffener, some cellophane tape to hold things together, and anything else handy around the house. Recycling is important today, so try to use items that might normally be discarded. Some kite contests award special prizes to the best kites made from recycled materials.

Your imagination can be your guide and the results can be great flying fun. Just one word of caution. It would probably be best to begin with construction of the more basic kite shapes, such as the kite shown in the next section of this book. Once you get the basic principles well in hand, then go on to the more exotic shapes and materials.

If you decide to buy a kite, try to visit one of the ever-increasing number of stores specializing in kites alone. You'll be astounded by the great splash of color as you walk in. There will be strange and beautiful kites hanging from every inch of the ceiling and on the walls. Dragons will stare down at you, fighting kites will tempt you to try this part of the sport, and old-time clipper ships will seem to plead with you to buy them and allow them to float on the air.

The longest kite in the world in 1978 was an astounding 400-foot model that still flies regularly at exhibitions. On one occasion it was flying as part

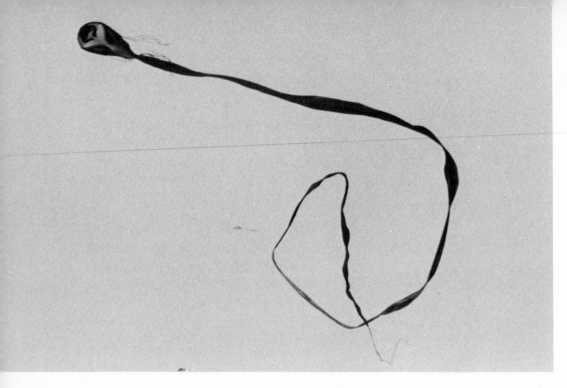

The 400-foot-long dragon kite during flight at Ontario Motor Speedway.

of the pre-race pageantry before an auto race at Ontario Motor Speedway in California. A part of a series of kites being pulled by cars down the nearly one-mile-long straightaway, the great black kite swooped and dipped, its tail looping around and around, at first swinging high in the air and out over the grandstands, then dipping to almost touch the track. The head of the kite, by then far down the track, seemed to continue on its own flight as its great tail followed far behind.

The tail would dip down and flick at the instruments of a band following the kite parade, or loop gently and carefully around the heads of pit workers. Then it would glide silently upward again until it was high in the air. In the slowly moving car, the flier would work the line this way and that to guide the great kite carefully so that it wouldn't tangle in the walls or wheel fences.

It was a fine demonstration, bringing cheers from the crowd.

TWO-STRING CONTROLLABLE KITES—Many, many modern kites have two strings for flying and controlling. The strings go all the way from the kite to the hand of the kite flyer. One string goes to one side of the kite, the other to the other side. By pulling one or the other, the flyer can cause the kite to fly in almost any direction. You will see these two-stringers at almost every kite festival and in a variety of styles and colors.

Bill Everett, an extraordinary kite flier, uses two reels to control his kite.

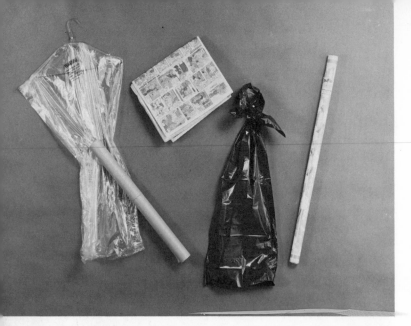

Basic kite building materials can usually be found around the house.

BUILDING A BASIC KITE

One of the greatest pleasures of kiting to many enthusiasts is to build a kite from scratch and then enjoy flying it. There, far up in the sky, is a creation you made yourself from spare parts. The parts may have been just so much junk before you started, and now they are proudly floating on the wind far above the ground.

It *is* a fine feeling. Nor is this a difficult matter to accomplish.

Here are some tips. Meanwhile, follow the illustrations carefully to see the real building of an Eddy-type kite from scratch.

1. Use bass, pine, or spruce, or even strong balsa wood for the bow stick and spine stick of a two-sticker kite. If you don't have any suitable pieces of wood around the house, a hobby store or kite shop can supply them in convenient sizes.

2. Cut a notch at each end of each stick (to

Notching the sticks can be done with a knife (very carefully) or with a small saw.

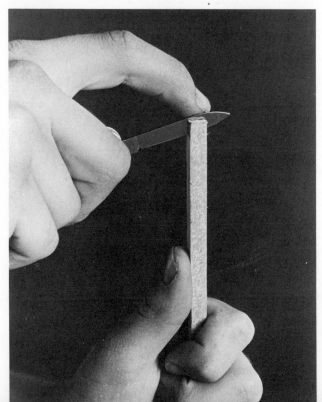

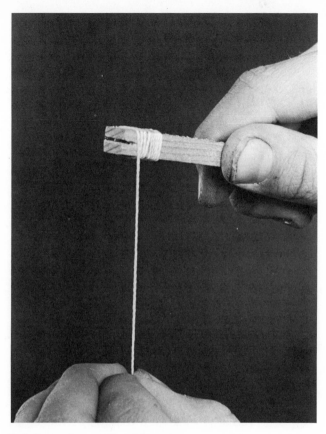

Reinforce the notch with string.

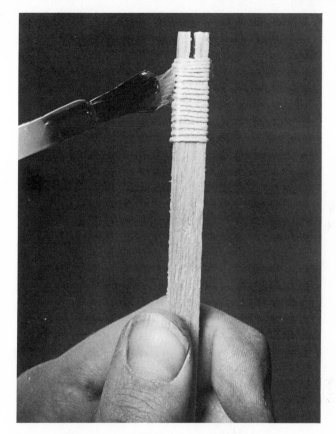

Glue on the string will hold the reinforcement.

accomodate the string frame you will later install), then reinforce each end by winding string tightly around the sticks just below where the notches have been cut.

3. Attach the center of the bow stick to the spine stick about 1/5 of the way down from the top of the spine. Do this by lashing the sticks together with string.

Tie the two sticks together with string, then reinforce with glue.

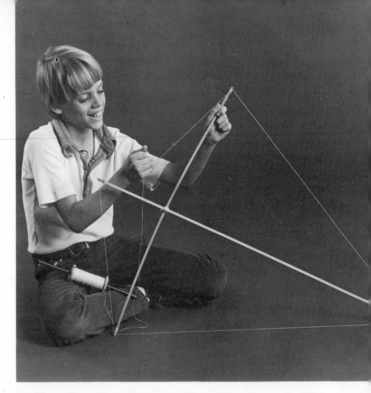

Outline the kite frame with string through the notches . . .

4. Attach a string to one end of the bow stick, then bend the bow stick until there is a distance of about 1/5 the length of the stick between the center of the stick and the string. Thus, if the stick is about 40 inches long, there should be a distance of about 8 inches between the string and the center of the bow stick. Tie the string tightly to the other end of the bow stick to maintain the bow.

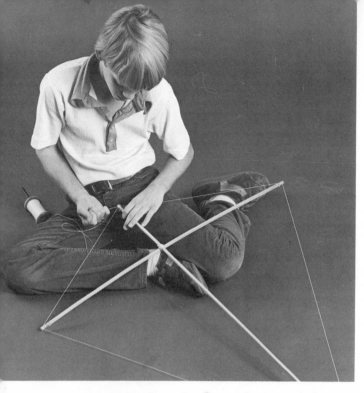

. . . and tie it off at the top or bottom of the vertical spar.

5. Now outline the kite with kite string, leading it through each notch in each stick and tying it at the bottom of the spine stick. Be sure the two sticks cross at right angles and that each side of the kite is exactly like the other side.

6. Cover the kite with your covering material (tissue paper, decorative paper, plastic, etc.) by first cutting the covering to size. Just lay it on the frame

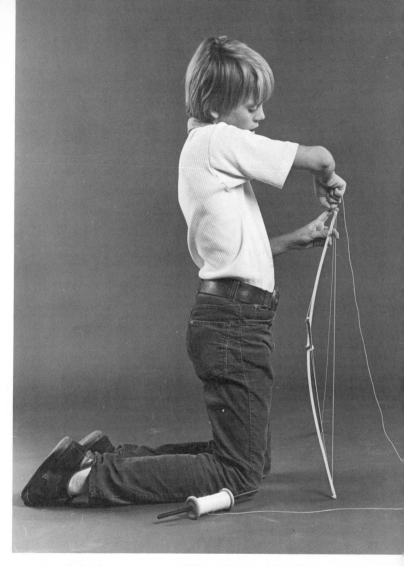

Now bend the bow stick carefully and tie with string.

Then outline the kite frame on the covering material. Below: Cut it to fit, with a one-inch overlap.

Glue the overlapping edges back upon themselves to mount the covering to the frame . . .

of the kite and cut around it, leaving one-inch extra all the way around. The covering will go on the bowed side, of course.

7. Turn the one-inch margin you have allowed back over the frame string and glue the margin to the covering.

8. Punch a small hole in the covering over the spine stick about halfway between the bow stick and the top of the spine stick. Tie the upper end of the bridle string to the spine stick, passing it through the covering. The lower end of the bridle should be tied to the bottom of the spine stick.

. . . and you have a basic Eddy-type kite.

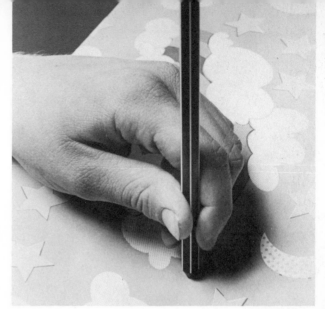

Above: Punch a hole in the covering over the vertical stick at the right location for the bridle string. **Below:** Install the bridle through the hole, then put a loop in the bridle to hold the flying string.

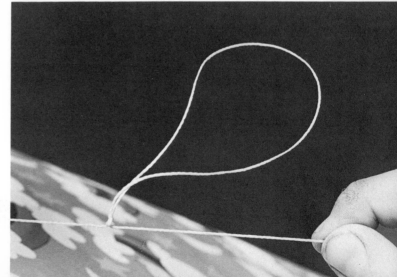

9. To locate the exact point where the flying line should be attached to the bridle, lay the bridle out flat on the surface of the kite, either to one side or the other. Align the top of the bridle with the bow stick. The bridle, if it is large enough, should reach out to the corner of the kite. Tie the flying string at this point.

10. The bridling point can be shifted up or down as you test the kite. Move it downward a fraction of an inch at a time if the kite rises too high and tends to dive and dip. Move it upward a fraction of an inch at a time if the kite does not want to rise to an angle of at least 65 degrees.

This kite will fly without a tail if it is properly balanced from side to side as this one is.

The bridle arrangement as described in the text.

Kit kites demand some modeling skill.

BUILDING KIT KITES

Will Yolen, an extraordinary kite flier and res-sponsible in a large measure for the popularity of kites in this country, did not prefer to design and build his own kites.

"Did Babe Ruth make his own bats?" Will would ask.

Yolen has a good point. Many, many kite fliers prefer to obtain a kite designed by somebody else, or a snap-together model readily available on the market, then concentrate on the fun of flying it. Such kites, in one form or another, are on the market

in such profusion that the problem becomes one of selecting the kite you want from those available.

But there are the two distinct types. You can buy a kit kite, one that will demand a fair amount of modeling skill to construct, or a snap-together model. There are about eight recognized kits on the market today. These are kits like the Fokker, the Sopwith Camel, the Ghost Clipper, the Wright Brothers' model, and others. Such kits do require

Squadron Kites are popular kit kites.

This scale model of the Wright brothers' first airplane is also popular.

Opposite: Assembling this delta-wing kite involves little more than inserting a dowel into plastic holders.

the modeling skill necessary to build any wood and paper airplane model. The average kit requires about 30 hours of construction time before flying, though expert modelers can accomplish the job in less time. Kits are for kite experts who enjoy building as well as flying.

Snap-together kites are much less time-consuming and generally much less expensive. Where a kit may require considerable time at home, a snap-together can be purchased, carried to the field, put together and flown. About all that may be required is snapping two sticks together, or attaching a bridle. They are easy to get ready for flight.

The illustrations show some of the modern kit kites and snap-together kites on the market today. There are hundreds of different models in the snap-together class, as a visit to any modern kite store will indicate.

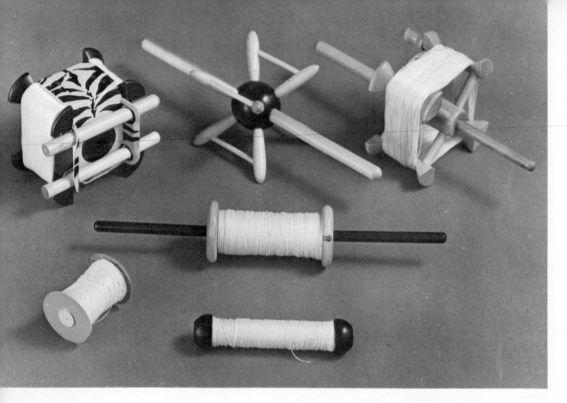

KITE FLYING SAFETY

For every sport or activity there are safety rules and cautions. You already know the first safety rule for kite flying: Never fly your kite in a thunderstorm. That can be very dangerous. As Ben Franklin proved, lightning can be attracted to the kite, passing electricity down the wet string.

Did you know that there is an international rule that covers kite flying? Nobody is allowed to fly anything that weighs more than 5 pounds to an altitude of more than 500 feet, unless prior permission has been obtained. (In the U.S. that permission would have to be obtained from the Federal Aviation Agency.) Kites and other objects are not allowed within a five-mile radius of any airport. The reason for these restrictions is so that air traffic is not endangered. If you are going for a record, or planning to fly a heavy kite high in the air for any reason, be sure to ask before launching.

MORE SAFETY RULES—Most safety rules are based on common sense.

1. Read the directions for building your kite before you begin. Some kites are tricky and require patience to get them ready to fly. If they are not constructed according to the directions, they won't fly properly and can be a danger to bystanders. A kite that dives into a crowd could injure somebody.

2. Never use metal in the building of a kite unless it is a special experimental kite being flown under strict conditions. Metal can attract lightning even if it isn't raining. Also, never use metallic string or wire as kite string, for the same reason. Even on a clear day, static electricity can build up and follow a kite string to the ground.

3. For all but the lightest kites, use gloves while flying. A rapidly moving string can cut into the skin of your hands.

4. Never fly a kite near telephone or power lines, or around a transmission tower. Kite fliers have been killed when their kites touched electric wires. If your kite should land on or near electric or telephone lines, don't try to retrieve it yourself. Ask your police or fire department for assistance.

Stay away from trees and buildings in flying a kite.

5. Never walk across a street or highway while flying a kite, or attempting to launch a kite. It is better to lose the kite than to endanger yourself, since your concentration will probably be on the kite and not on your surroundings.

6. For the safety of your kite, remember that if it is going in the wrong direction (into a tree, for example) let out on the line until it is pointing in the direction you want it to go. Then gently haul in.

Model rocketeers, who also launch objects into the air, have come to be wary of a certain type of tree. They call it "Hibranchus catchanholdem." Kite fliers must also be aware of the deadly *H. catchanholdem*, and fly away from it. Most trees fit into this "scientific" category.

There is the story about the man who was out flying a kite for his children. He had picked a large meadow that rose gently to a knoll upon which one small tree was growing. Surely he could avoid that one single tree.

No. After a time the kite dropped and looped its string over the tallest branch of the little tree. The kite was hanging, turning gently in the slight breeze, only about nine feet off the ground. The line had looped around a single little twig higher up, and there the matter stood.

The man tried to reach the kite by jumping. He was sure if he grabbed the kite, the twig would break and the kite would be undamaged. But on one of his mighty leaps, he not only missed the kite again, but when he landed he twisted his ankle. The injury was very painful. There seemed no answer but for someone to call an ambulance, since he couldn't walk.

That didn't end the story though. As the attendants were carrying the man back down the slight hill, they were getting the story of how the accident had happened. The man's children told the story in such a way that the ambulance men began to chuckle. One thing led to another and the stretcher tipped over. When the man fell out, he broke his arm.

Not the fault of kite flying, perhaps, but it does show how one thing can lead to another and make an otherwise safe activity painfully unsafe. It also shows that *H. catchanholdem* comes in all sizes, shapes, and varieties and can cause problems in strange ways.

There are other dangers. In 1973 a helicopter was forced to make an emergency landing because of a kite. The kite had broken free and finally its line tangled in a tree near the Norfolk Naval Air Station in Virginia. So it remained in the air too near the flight pattern to ignore. The helicopter was sent to cut the string of the kite and cause it to fall. But the line tangled in the helicopter's blade and the aircraft had to quickly land.

Many times kite strings have fallen across power lines and cut off power because of a short circuit.

The all-time record was probably the time a kite string fell across a high power line near Texarkana, Texas. The resulting short circuit cut off power to more than 10,000 homes and knocked two radio stations off the air.

H. catchanholdem **in action.**

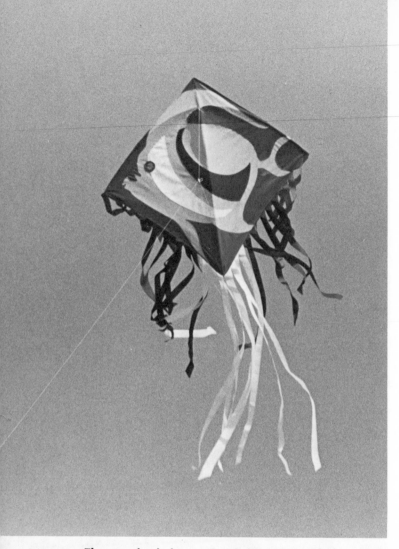

The standard shape of a fighting kite. The streamers are decorations and not used when fighting.

KITE FIGHTING

Kite fighting is a national pastime in such countries as China, Japan, Korea, India, and other Far Eastern and Asian lands. They have been flying kites in these countries for thousands of years and kites are a familiar part of the social structure.

In China a traditional celebration with kites was held on the ninth day of the ninth month of the year. Hundreds of years ago a Chinese man had a vision of danger to his family on that certain day. So he took his family to a nearby hill for an all-day picnic and there they stayed together, flying their kites. When he returned home, he found his house destroyed by fire and his animals all buried in the rubble. Each year after that he took his household kite flying on that day to celebrate the saving of his family, and the festival spread throughout China.

In Japan, there is a Boys' Festival and on this day every household flies a kite shaped like a carp fish in honor of each son. The carp is a symbol for courage in Japan. Many American communities have kite flying festivals and tournaments where awards are given for the highest flying kite, the most beautiful kite, the kite that pulls the hardest, the most unusual kite, the best home-built kite, and other categories. There is one special category—kite fighting—that is fairly new to this country but growing rapidly in popularity. However, it is a form of kite flying well known to citizens of many other countries.

Famous kite fighter Vic Heredia in proper kite fighting stance.

KITE FIGHTING—A kite fighting duel can be like something straight out of the Old West, or it can be a formal, regulated contest like many held throughout the year. You can just challenge somebody and fight, or you can sign in where a regular contest is being held. Either way can be very exciting.

There is a story about the famous kite flier, Will Yolen. Yolen is one of the leading forces in kite flying in the United States. He became the Western Hemisphere Kite Flying Champion after defeating the Maharaja of Bharapur in a long battle in 1961, while visiting in India. Yolen is an expert.

One of his greatest battles, though, was in New York City. Some of Yolen's kite flying friends from Harlem complained to him about a lone kite fighter working off the roof of a building. The lone fighter's kite string was equipped with razor blades, and he delighted in cutting down any kites flown in the neighborhood.

That is the point of a kite fight. You must maneuver your kite into position to cut the flying string of another kite. Normally you use a coated cutting string, but not this lone fighter. Soon he became known as the Razor Blade Man.

Yolen allowed word to go out that he was challenging Razor Blade Man to a winner-take-all kite fight. It would be one-on-one, with the duel to go on until the last kite was down. The challenge was accepted. The place would be Central Park.

Both fighters arrived with their best fighting kites and the battle began. They were evenly matched

In kite fighting, the idea is to remove your opponent's kite from the sky.

and the day wore on as kite after kite dodged around and finally fluttered to the ground. It was afternoon, then early evening, and still the two battled to a stand-off. The next kite would be the last kite and would decide the winner.

Yolen was a strategist. He knew something that perhaps Razor Blade Man didn't. On other evenings in Central Park, as dusk approached, Yolen had noted a slackening of the wind. Counting on this, he flew his fighting kite far over the other just as the wind died. Diving without mercy on the sagging kite of his opponent, Yolen sliced through the string cleanly and the battle was won.

Kite fighting contests are called "penches." There are three types.

One-against-one, group-against-group (with ten to each team as a general rule), and the best of all to most fighters and spectators, open-air fights. Rules for kite fighting are very intricate in India and other Eastern countries, but such rules can also be informal. They can be whatever the contestants agree to beforehand.

The idea, in the end, is to cut the string of your opponent's kite with your own cutting string.

THE CUTTING STRING—Fighting kites have a cutting string about 100-feet long. This line is attached to the bridle of the kite. Then the flying string, ordinary cotton line, is attached to the cutting string. Cutting string can be purchased at most kite stores. Called *Manjha* in India, it is ordinary cotton line coated with a paste of powdered glass, egg, and starch. The line is coated and then stretched between poles to dry. Wet, it is harmless, but once dry, the cutting string has thousands of tiny sharp edges used to slice or saw through another kite string.

Some fighters double-coat their cutting string. The single-coated line cuts in only one direction, but the double-coated line cuts from above or below and can be used to slice (by pulling in on the flying line) or saw (by letting out on the flying line). Legend says that in India, where kite fighting is a national sport, wealthy fighters coated their cutting strings with diamond dust.

Be careful with the cutting line of a fighting kite. If you do not handle it properly it can cut your fingers (or nearby spectators).

A PENCH—A contest between kite fighters may last only a few minutes, and involve only one kite, or it may last several hours. Each time a kite string is cut in a formal contest, the loser puts up another kite. This means that the winner must use another section of the cutting string to cut, since one section has been worn away with the last cut. More than three cuts with one cutting string is good. Nine cuts with one string rates a special trophy in formal contests.

In a formal match, fifteen minutes is set aside at the beginning of each hour for replacement of the cutting string. Most experts replace the entire string, both cutting and flying parts, at this time.

There is a flying circle inside which the fighter must remain during the pench. The circle is about ten feet in diameter. Circles for other fighters must be at least twenty feet away. No fighter may leave his or her circle during the pench.

Although the normal number of players on a kite fighting team is ten, any number can play as long as each side is equal. The rules are about the same, but in team fighting each team has kites of a certain color so that team members can quickly tell their own kites from those of the other team.

Open-air fighting is one-on-one with anybody attacking anybody within range. You and your kite are on your own, against the world. There are open-air contests in Eastern countries where the sky is dotted with kites, where thousands upon thousands of kites are involved. Fighters rarely see their opponents. They only see the kites. Sometimes they cannot even see their own kite in the mass of colorful darting confusion overhead.

Expert kite fighters learn to tell how their kite is doing and exactly when to slice or saw their cutting string by the feel of the flying string in their hands. They know without seeing that their cutting string is across the line of another kite.

HOW TO FIGHT A KITE—There are kite fighting countries where razor blades, sharp knives tied to tails, and other wicked devices are legal in a pench. The idea is to remove your opponent's kite from the sky by any means possible.

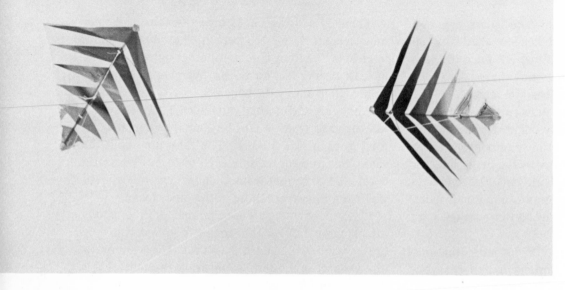

Most kite fighters use coated cutting strings for more than reasons of rules or safety. The cutting string technique demands the greatest kite flying skill. Extra objects on the kite might fall into the crowd, seriously injuring somebody. There is a beauty to kite fighting that goes beyond slashing and crashing and destroying.

With the coating string technique, the secret is in the way you hold and handle the flying line. The most sensitive part of your forefinger is about three-quarters of an inch from the tip, on the underside. Hold the flying string between the thumb and this section of your forefinger and soon you will be able to feel even very slight pressure changes as your cutting string crosses that of an opponent.

If you keep your fighting kite as close as possible to the one of your opponent, you will be using the upper section of your cutting string. You cut an opponent's line by a quick up and down motion, letting out, then pulling in, as your cutting string crosses the other. As you do this, cause your kite to dive and increase the pressure of your string against your opponent's.

It is also possible to cut from underneath as your cutting string rises up to touch the other line. If this should happen, fly your kite so that it is aiming

straight up, then pay out your flying line so that your cutting string works upward from under the other string.

If you are a beginner to this exciting sport, fly more than the suggested twenty feet away from your opponent. The greater the distance, the better the angle when the two strings cross. If you fly thirty, forty, or fifty feet away, and both of you keep your kites low (perhaps 100 feet or so) you will more quickly learn the techniques of kite fighting.

Maneuvering a fighting kite is not difficult. You can make it go right or left by giving the flying string a quick jerk then letting out a few feet of line. This will cause the kite to rotate. Watch the nose of the kite and when it is heading in the direction you have chosen, pull in hard. As long as you keep pulling in, the kite will continue in that direction.

There are several factors which will determine the ultimate victor in a kite fight.

1. The wind
2. The controllability of your kite
3. The height of your kite
4. The size and weight of your kite
5. The sensitivity of your fingers
6. Experience

If you are more clever than your opponent and have equipment you have learned to use, you will win. But if your opponent is also very good and very experienced and with equipment that is also good, the fight will go on and on. It is very exciting. Sooner

or later one of you will make a mistake and suddenly one kite will flutter sadly to the ground.

Some experts have become so skillful that they can achieve the ultimate victory. They can capture the other kite and bring it down to their own circle. Once the vanquished kite's string is totally parted, they streak in and begin to loop around and around the trailing string. Soon the two strings are tangled and the kite can be pulled in.

It has happened that a fighter attempts to bring in a kite and the trailing cutting string cuts the winners' own string. Then both kites fall to the ground. So beware. You have already won when you cut the string. Too much show business can get you into serious trouble if you don't know exactly what you are doing.

KITE FIGHTING THE AMERICAN WAY—You have read about kite fighting the way it is done in Eastern countries, and by many kite fighters in the United States. There are other fighters, however, who do not enjoy the sight of a kite fluttering to the ground. They do not like losing their kites when a breeze carries them far from the fighting area.

Perhaps most important, they are concerned about the safety hazard a cutting string presents. Such a string in the wrong hands can be dangerous. One child in bare feet tripped over an abandoned cutting string and was cut to the bone. Still, if a fight is conducted with cutting strings, many yards of the string are certain to be lost. At the very least, cutting

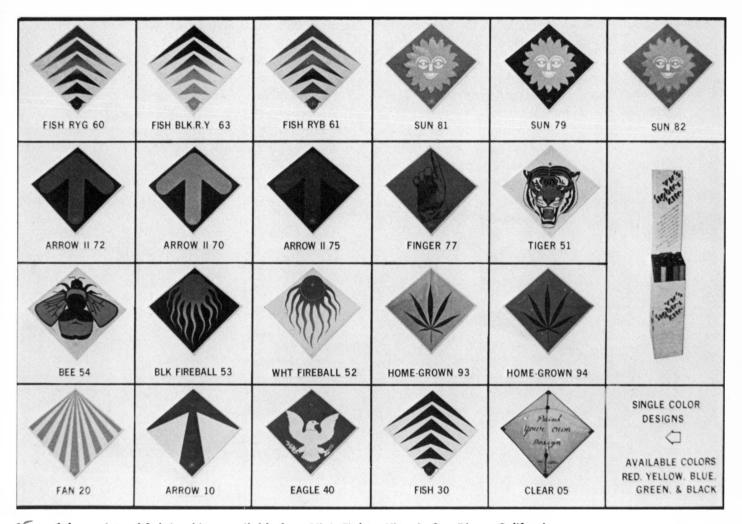

FISH RYG 60	FISH BLK.R.Y 63	FISH RYB 61	SUN 81	SUN 79	SUN 82
ARROW II 72	ARROW II 70	ARROW II 75	FINGER 77	TIGER 51	
BEE 54	BLK FIREBALL 53	WHT FIREBALL 52	HOME-GROWN 93	HOME-GROWN 94	
FAN 20	ARROW 10	EAGLE 40	FISH 30	CLEAR 05	SINGLE COLOR DESIGNS — AVAILABLE COLORS RED. YELLOW. BLUE. GREEN. & BLACK

Some of the variety of fighting kites available from Vic's Fighter Kites in San Diego, California.

string can drift down among spectators. They could be people who do not know of the danger of the string.

So American fighters have devised a new way to get just as much fun from fighting with kites.

They use the same type of kites, but they do not use cutting string. Instead, they attach a short (about three or four feet) tail made of crepe paper. The idea then becomes to see who can cut the tail from another kite. This can be done with the kite body or with the kite string. The crepe paper cuts off easily. It does not add much weight at all, and the activity becomes much safer for everybody.

Yes, sometimes a kite is knocked from the sky by an overzealous fighter, but the modern kite fighter prefers this to cutting strings littering the area. All of the control techniques still apply to this newer way to fight.

FOR MORE INFORMATION

Captain Kite
River City Kite Works
P.O. Box 26202
Sacramento, CA   95826

Come Fly A Kite
900 N. Point
Ghirardelli Square
San Francisco, CA   94109

Coventry Sales
1811½ Coventry Road
Cleveland Heights, OH   44118

Flying Tiger Associates (reels)
P.O. Box 48634
Los Angeles, CA   90048

Gayla Industries
P.O. Box 10800
Houston, TX   77081

Grandmaster Kites
P.O. Box 12377
Portland, OR   97212

Great Winds
166 S. Jackson Street
Seattle, WA   98104

Go Fly A Kite
1434 Third Avenue
New York, NY   10028

The Hi-Flier Manufacturing Co.
510 East Wabash
Decatur, IL   62525

High As A Kite
691 Bridgeway
Sausalito, CA   94965

International Kite Co.
P.O. Box 3248
San Diego, CA   92103

Kites, Kites, Kites
P.O. Box 845
Bowie, MD   20715

The Kite Company
33 West Orange
Chagrin Falls, OH   44022

The Kite Factory
P.O. Box 9081
Seattle, WA   98109

The Kite Site
3101 M Street
Georgetown, DC   20007

The Kite Shop, Ltd.
1917 Kalakaua Avenue
Honolulu, HI   96815

Lee's Kites
3902 41st Avenue
Seattle, WA   98116

Let's Fly A Kite
13763 Fiji Way
Marina del Rey, CA   90291

Marblehead Kite Company
P.O. Box 961
Marblehead, MA   01945

Nantucket Kiteman and Lady
P.O. Box 1356
Nantucket, MA   02554

Quicksilver Kites
701 Shrader Street
San Francisco, CA   94117

Rafco
3136 Kashiwa Street
Torrance, CA   90505

Rainbow Kite Co.
26 Park Avenue
Venice, CA   90291

Rogallo Flexkites
Kitty Hawk, NC   27949

Satellite Kites
1729-H Woodland Avenue
Palo Alto, CA   94303

Skyworks
Old Verbank Road
Millbrook, NY   12545

Sports Innovations
P.O. Box 385
Wichita Falls, TX   76307

Stratton Air Engineering
10859 Portal Drive
Los Alamitos, CA   90721

Spectra Star Kites
3519 Caribeth
Encino, CA   91436

Synestructics, Inc.
9400 Lurline Avenue
Chatsworth, CA   91311

Ultra Kite
904 Centura Building
Pittsburgh, PA   15222

Vancouver Kites and Crafts
2936 W. 4th Street
Vancouver, BC, Canada

Veekay International
4784 Briarbend Trace
Stone Mountain, GA   30088

Vic's Fighter Kites
3260 F Street
San Diego, CA   92102

W.O. Weather & Sons (reels)
17707 S.E. Howard Street
Milwaukie, OR   97222

What's Up
4500 Chagrin River Road
Chagrin Falls, OH   44022

Zenith Kites
P.O. Box 99413
San Francisco, CA   94109

INDEX

Ross R. Olney is the author of dozens of sports books for younger readers, many of them about cars and motor racing. But he also writes about hockey, football, soccer, baseball, and science subjects. His latest book for Dodd, Mead is *Modern Motorcycle Superstars*. Olney is a full-time author and part-time hang glider, skin diver, sailor, and camper. He lives with his lawyer wife and two younger sons in Ventura, California.

Chan Bush is a photographer of national prominence. His studio in Los Angeles is well known for the advertising and sports photography he has done. Over 350 covers on a variety of national magazines have the Bush credit line. He and Olney have collaborated on several other books since their meeting in 1960. Bush lives in La Crescenta, California, with his wife and three children.